Differentiated Reading
for Comprehension

Grade 4

Credits

Content Editor: Christine Schwab
Copy Editor: Karen Seberg
Illustrations: Nick Greenwood, Donald O'Connor

Visit carsondellosa.com for correlations to Common Core, state, national, and Canadian provincial standards.

Carson-Dellosa Publishing, LLC
PO Box 35665
Greensboro, NC 27425 USA
carsondellosa.com

ISBN 978-1-4838-0489-7

01-034141151

Table of Contents

Introduction

Providing all students access to high quality, nonfiction text is essential to Common Core State Standards mastery. This book contains exactly what teachers are looking for: high-interest nonfiction passages, each written at three different reading levels, followed by a shared set of text-dependent comprehension questions and a writing prompt to build content knowledge. Both general academic and domain-specific vocabulary words are reinforced at the end of each passage for further comprehension support. The standards listed on each page provide an easy reference tool for lesson planning and the Common Core Alignment chart on page 3 allows you to target or remediate specific skills.

The book is comprised of 15 stories that are written at three levels:
- Below level (one dot beside the page number): 1 to 1.5 levels below grade level
- On level (two dots beside the page number): 0 to .5 levels below grade level
- Advanced (three dots beside the page number): 1 to 2 levels above grade level

Which students will not enjoy reading about a 200-pound (90.71 kg) lizard or the mysterious Loch Ness Monster or how Anne Frank hid for two years behind a bookcase? This will quickly become the go-to resource for differentiated nonfiction reading practice in your classroom!

Common Core Alignment Chart

Common Core State Standards*		Practice Pages
Reading Standards for Informational Text		
Key Ideas and Details	4.RI.1–4.RI.3	7, 11, 15, 19, 23, 27, 31, 35, 39, 43, 47, 51, 55, 59
Craft and Structure	4.RI.4–4.RI.6	4–6, 7, 8–10, 11, 12–14, 15, 16–18, 19, 20–22, 24–26, 28–30, 31, 32–34, 36–38, 39, 40–42, 43, 44–46, 47, 48–50, 52–54, 56–58, 60–62
Integration of Knowledge and Ideas	4.RI.7–4.RI.9	19, 23, 59, 63
Range of Reading and Level of Text Complexity	4.RI.10	4–6, 8–10, 12–14, 16–18, 20–22, 24–26, 28–30, 32–34, 36–38, 40–42, 44–46, 48–50, 52–54, 56–58, 60–62
Reading Standards: Foundational Skills		
Phonics and Word Recognition	4.RF.3	43, 63
Fluency	4.RF.4	4–6, 8–10, 11, 12–14, 16–18, 20–22, 24–26, 28–30, 32–34, 36–38, 40–42, 44–46, 48–50, 52–54, 56–58, 60–62, 63
Writing Standards		
Text Types and Purposes	4.W.1–4.W.3	7, 11, 15, 19, 23, 31, 35, 39, 43, 47, 55, 59, 63
Production and Distribution of Writing	4.W.4–4.W.6	27, 31, 51
Language Standards		
Conventions of Standard English	4.L.1–4.L.2	7, 19, 47, 51, 55, 63
Knowledge of Language	4.L.3	23
Vocabulary Acquisition and Use	4.L.4–4.L.6	4–6, 8–10, 11, 12–14, 15, 16–18, 20–22, 23, 24–26, 27, 28–30, 32–34, 35, 36–38, 40–42, 44–46, 48–50, 51, 52–54, 55, 56–58, 59, 60–62

How to Use This Alignment Chart

The Common Core State Standards for English Language Arts are a shared set of expectations for each grade level in the areas of reading, writing, speaking, listening, and language. They define what students should understand and be able to do. This chart presents the standards that are covered in this book.

Use this chart to plan your instruction, practice, or remediation of a specific standard. To do this, first choose your targeted standard; then, find the pages listed on the chart that correlate to the standard you are teaching. Finally, assign the reading pages and follow-up questions to practice the skill.

Brilliant Bait

Have you ever seen a **clown fish**? You probably have. The clown fish has bright stripes and colors just like a clown. That is probably where it got its name. There are many different patterns and colors on the bodies of clown fish. The most common is orange with white and black stripes.

A real clown fish is not funny. The clown fish is a fish to be feared. It protects its home and its eggs with care. The female clown fish lays between 300 and 700 eggs at one time. But, the male clown fish takes care of the eggs. He watches them until they hatch. One strange thing about clown fish is that they can change gender. If a female dies or is killed, the male can change into a female in a few weeks. Then, it mates with a male and keeps laying eggs.

The clown fish has a strange home. It lives in the **tentacles**, or arms, of a sea animal called an **anemone**. These two animals have made a deal with each other. The anemone doesn't eat the clown fish and provides a safe home. In return, the clown fish does three things for the anemone. It cleans the anemone's tentacles, eating leftover bits of food. It guards the anemone against some enemies. And, it acts as bait. The clown fish's bright stripes draw other fish to the deadly tentacles. The anemone stings these fish and eats them. The "friendship" between these two sea animals works very well for both of them.

Where in the world does the clown fish live? It can be found in the seas near India, Indonesia, and Australia. Each bright, strong little fish always lives with the same sea anemone, never leaving its side.

clown fish: a small tropical fish that is bright orange, usually with one or more white stripes

tentacles: arms that usually lead from the head or around the mouth of animals

anemone: a sea animal whose body is surrounded by petal-like tentacles

Brilliant Bait

Have you ever seen a **clown fish**? You probably have. The clown fish has bright stripes and colors just like a clown. That is probably where it got its name. There are many different patterns and colors on the bodies of clown fish. The most common is orange with white and black stripes.

A real clown fish is not funny. The clown fish is a fierce fish, a fish to be feared. It protects its home and its eggs with care. The female clown fish lays between 300 and 700 eggs at one time. But, the male clown fish takes care of the eggs. He watches them until they hatch. One strange thing about clown fish is that they can change gender. If a female dies or is killed, the male can change into a female in a few weeks. Then, it mates with a male and keeps laying eggs.

The clown fish has a strange home. It lives in the **tentacles**, or arms, of a sea animal called an **anemone**. These two animals have made a deal with each other. The anemone doesn't eat the clown fish and provides a safe home. In return, the clown fish does three things for the anemone. It cleans the anemone's tentacles, eating leftover bits of food. It guards the anemone against some enemies. And, it acts as bait. The clown fish's bright stripes draw other fish to the deadly tentacles. The anemone stings these fish and eats them. The "friendship" between these two sea animals works very well for both of them.

Where in the world does the clown fish live? It can be found in the seas near India, Indonesia, and Australia. Each bright, strong little fish always lives with the same sea anemone, never leaving its side.

clown fish: a small tropical fish that is bright orange, usually with one or more white stripes

tentacles: arms that usually lead from the head or around the mouth of animals, especially invertebrates

anemone: a sea animal whose body is surrounded by petal-like tentacles

Brilliant Bait

Have you ever seen a **clown fish**? You probably have and recognize it as Nemo from the movie called *Finding Nemo.* This interesting and colorful fish is also known as the clown anemonefish. Its **genus name** is *Amphiprion.* The clown fish has wide, bright stripes and distinctive colors that resemble the costume of a clown. That is probably where it got its name. There are many different patterns and colors on the bodies of clown fish. The most common coloration is orange with white and black stripes.

A real clown fish is not amusing like its namesake. The clown fish is a fierce and **vigilant** fish. It protects its home and its eggs with great care. The female clown fish lays between 300 and 700 eggs at one time. But, the male clown fish takes care of the eggs. He watches them until they hatch. One strange and interesting thing about clown fish is that they can change gender. If a female dies or is killed, the male can change into a female in a few weeks. Then, it mates with a male and keeps laying eggs.

The clown fish has an unusual home. It lives in the tentacles, or arms, of a multicolored sea animal called an **anemone**. These two animals have struck a deal with each other in order to accommodate each other's needs. The anemone doesn't eat the clown fish and provides protection and a safe home. In return, the clown fish does three things for the anemone. It cleans the anemone's tentacles, eating whatever leftover bits of food lodge there. It also guards the anemone against its predators. And lastly, it acts as bait. The clown fish's bright stripes draw other fish to the deadly tentacles of the anemone. The anemone stings these fish and eats them. The odd and unlikely "friendship" between these two sea animals benefits them both.

Where in the world does the clown fish live? It can be found in the seas near India, Indonesia, and Australia. Each bright, strong little fish always lives with the same sea anemone, never leaving its side. They are partners for life.

clown fish: a small tropical fish that is bright orange usually with one or more white stripes
genus name: labels a class, kind, or group with common characteristics
vigilant: alert, particularly to avoid danger
anemone: a sea animal whose body is surrounded by petal-like tentacles

Name _Robert_

Brilliant Bait

Answer the questions.

1. How many eggs can a female clown fish lay at one time? Write your answer in a complete sentence.

   A Female fish can lay up to 300-700 eggs a one time

2. Choose the word that best completes this sentence:

   Another word for tentacles is _____.

   A. spurs   **B.** hands   **C. arms** (circled)   **D.** eyes

Write **T** for true or **F** for false.

3. __T__ The clown fish can change gender.

4. __F__ A female clown fish lays 5,000 eggs at a time.

5. __F__ Anemones kill clown fish for food.

6. __T__ The anemone uses its tentacles to sting fish.

7. __F__ All clown fish are orange with white and black stripes.

8. Which of the following does not describe the clown fish?

   A. brightly colored   **B.** timid   **C. funny** (circled)   **D.** B. and C.

9. Finish the sentences to list the three things that a clown fish does for a sea anemone.

   A. It cleans the anemone's _tentacles_ .

   B. It guards the anemone against _it's preditors_ .

   C. It acts as _bait_ to attract food for the anemone.

10. How did the clown fish probably get its name? Write your answer in a complete sentence.

    It probally got it's name because they are colorful just like real clowns

11. What is the main idea of this story? What details help you answer this question?

    I think it's about how clown fish live and what life is like for them

12. Imagine you are deep underwater looking at the bottom of the ocean. On a separate sheet of paper, describe what you might see.

Wow! That's Fast!

Your heart beats about 72 times a minute. The heart of a hummingbird beats 17 times faster! A hummingbird's heart beats about 1,260 times a minute.

The hummingbird does almost everything fast. It can fly up to 60 miles per hour (96.56 kmh). Its wings beat 75 times a second. You can hardly see a hummingbird's wings when it flies by. They are a **blur**.

This fast bird is the smallest bird in the world. Most hummingbirds are only about three inches (7.62 cm) long. Some are smaller. Hummingbird eggs are the size of green peas. These tiny birds are so small that they can be killed by a bee sting!

A hummingbird's nest is also tiny. It is only about two inches (5.08 cm) wide. The female hummingbird makes her nest from spiderwebs. Then, she puts moss on the outside of the sticky nest. This makes the nest hard to see.

The hummingbird has a long beak. But, it has no sense of smell. It uses its eyes to find flowers. Then, it laps up the **nectar** from the flowers. It uses its long, split tongue to do this. The bird has to drink its body weight in nectar every day, or it will die. This is because it uses so much energy for flying. It also eats tiny bugs.

People once thought that hummingbirds did not have feet. They never saw a hummingbird **perch**. The hummingbird has to perch many times a day to rest. But, this tiny, fast bird perches so quickly that people might not see it.

blur: something moving too quickly to be seen clearly
nectar: a sweet liquid from a plant
perch: to sit or rest

Wow! That's Fast!

The human heart beats about 72 times every minute. If you were a hummingbird, your heart would beat 17 times faster! When it is flying, a hummingbird's heart beats about 1,260 times every minute.

In fact, the hummingbird does almost everything fast. It is a superbird! It can fly up to 60 miles per hour (96.56 kmh). Its wings beat 75 times every second. When a hummingbird flies by you, you can hardly see its wings. They are a **blur**, a flash of color that is gone before your eyes know what they saw.

All of this incredible speed is found in the smallest bird in the world. Most hummingbirds are only about three inches (7.62 cm) long, and some are even tinier. Hummingbird eggs are **minute**, the size of green peas. These thumb-size birds are so small that they can be killed by a bee sting!

A hummingbird's nest is also tiny. It is only about two inches (5.08 cm) wide. The female hummingbird makes her nest from spiderwebs. Then, she puts moss on the sticky outside of the nest. This makes the nest hard for enemies to see.

The hummingbird has a long beak, but it has no sense of smell. It uses its eyes to find flowers. Then, it laps up the **nectar** from the flowers. It uses its long, split tongue to do this. The bird has to drink its body weight in nectar every day, or it will die. This is because it uses so much energy for flying. It also eats tiny bugs.

Long ago, people thought that hummingbirds did not have feet. They never saw a hummingbird **perch**. In fact, the hummingbird has to perch many times a day to save its energy. But, like everything else that this tiny, swift bird does, it perches so quickly that people might not see it.

blur: something moving too quickly to be seen clearly
minute: very small
nectar: thick juice from a fruit
perch: to sit or rest

Wow! That's Fast!

The human heart beats about 72 times every minute. If you were a hummingbird, your heart would beat 17 times faster! When it is flying, a hummingbird's heart beats about 1,260 times every minute. That is about 21 beats in the **brief** second it takes to say *hummingbird*.

In fact, the hummingbird is speedy at practically everything. It can fly up to 60 miles per hour (96.56 kmh), which is about how fast people drive on highways. Its wings beat 75 times every second. When a hummingbird flies by you, you can hardly see its wings. They are a **blur**, a flash of color.

All of this speed is found in the smallest bird in the world. Most hummingbirds are only about three inches (7.62 cm) long, and some are even smaller. Hummingbird eggs are **minute**, the size of green peas. These tiny birds are so small that they can be killed by a bee sting!

A hummingbird's nest looks miniature when compared to other bird nests. It is only a scant two inches (5.08 cm) wide. The female hummingbird makes her nest from spiderwebs. Then, she puts clumps of moss on the sticky outer edges of the nest. This makes the nest difficult for predators to detect.

The hummingbird has a long, narrow beak, but it has no sense of smell. It uses its keen eyesight to locate flowers. Then, it laps up the nectar, or sweet juice, from the flowers. It uses its long, split tongue to do this. The bird has to drink its body weight in nectar every day, or it will die. This is because it uses so much energy for flying. It also eats tiny bugs.

Long ago, people thought that hummingbirds did not have feet. They never saw a hummingbird perch, or sit. In fact, however, the hummingbird must perch many times a day to **conserve** its energy. But, like everything else that this tiny, swift bird does, it perches so quickly that people might rarely see it.

brief: short in duration
blur: something moving too quickly to be seen clearly
minute: very small
conserve: to use carefully to prevent loss

Wow! That's Fast!

Answer the questions.

1. The title "Wow! That's Fast!" refers to
   - **A.** the human heartbeat
   - **B.** the heartbeat of a hummingbird
   - **C.** the life span of a hummingbird
   - **D.** all of the above

2. Read the following sentence from the story and answer the question.

   But, like everything else that this tiny, swift bird does, it perches so quickly that people might rarely see it.

   What is a synonym for *swift*?
   - **A.** cute
   - **B.** thoughtful
   - **C.** fast
   - D. slow

3. Choose the best description of the hummingbird.
   - **A.** a bird with a very fast heartbeat
   - **B.** a bird that flies very fast
   - **C.** a very fast bird that is the smallest bird in the world
   - **D.** a bird that lays very small eggs

4. Why did people once think that hummingbirds did not have feet? Write your answer in a complete sentence.

   _____

5. Write three words or phrases from the story that tell about a hummingbird's size.

   _____   _____   _____

6. Why does a hummingbird have to eat so much every day?
   - **A.** It needs to lay eggs.
   - **B.** It needs to perch on branches.
   - **C.** It needs to make nests from spiderwebs.
   - **D.** It uses so much energy when it flies.

7. Circle the three phrases that best describe features of the hummingbird.

   fast wings   large feet   pea-sized eggs   short beak   split tongue   very still

8. Describe hummingbirds using two similes or metaphors.

   _____

9. What is the main idea of the story? What details help you answer this question?

   _____

10. On a separate sheet of paper, write a paragraph that compares the hummingbird to a bird of a different size, the eagle. Use information from this text and other sources.

Living Large, Lizard Style

Imagine a lizard big enough to kill a buffalo. Is this science fiction? Not in Indonesia, where the **Komodo dragon** lives. It can grow to be up to 10 feet (3.05 m) long and 200 pounds (90.72 kg). The Komodo dragon is good at hunting. It has no enemies.

The Komodo dragon has **stubby** legs, but it can run fast. Sometimes, it doesn't have to. If a Komodo dragon bites another animal, the animal will start to die. That's because the Komodo dragon has **bacteria** in its mouth. After biting its **prey**, the Komodo dragon walks slowly behind the animal until it drops to the ground.

This giant lizard also has a good sense of smell. A Komodo dragon tastes the air with its tongue. It can smell animals up to five miles (8.05 km) away. It has sharp claws and even sharper teeth. Its teeth are jagged and look like shark teeth. These teeth break off easily. Then, the Komodo dragon just grows more.

The Komodo dragon will eat another Komodo dragon's eggs. A mother has to work hard to hide her eggs. First, she digs a hole three feet (91.44 cm) deep. Then, she lays 30 eggs at one time. She quickly buries them so that they do not get eaten.

When the little Komodo dragons hatch, they dig out of the sand. They run as fast as they can for the trees. Adult Komodo dragons cannot climb trees. The baby Komodo dragons live in the trees for at least two years. The babies live on insects, birds, and bird eggs. They only climb down from the trees when they can take care of themselves.

Komodo dragon: the largest of all known lizards
stubby: short and thick
bacteria: poisonous germs
prey: an animal taken for food

Living Large, Lizard Style

Imagine a lizard big enough to kill a buffalo. Science fiction? Not in Indonesia, where the **Komodo dragon** lives. This lizard can grow to be up to 10 feet (3.05 m) long and 200 pounds (90.72 kg). The Komodo dragon is so good at hunting that it is at the top of its food chain. It has no enemies.

The Komodo dragon has many features that help it hunt. It has **stubby** legs, but it can run fast. Sometimes, it doesn't have to. If a Komodo dragon bites another animal, the prey will start to die. That's because the Komodo dragon has bacteria, or poisonous germs, in its mouth. After biting its **prey**, the Komodo dragon walks slowly behind the animal until it drops to the ground.

This giant lizard also has a keen sense of smell. A Komodo dragon actually tastes the air with its forked tongue. It can use its tongue to smell animals up to five miles (8.05 km) away. It has sharp claws and even sharper teeth. Its teeth are jagged. These teeth break off easily, but if they do, the Komodo dragon just grows more.

The Komodo dragon will eat its own kind. It will also eat another Komodo dragon's eggs. A mother has to work hard to hide her eggs. First, she digs a hole three feet (91.44 cm) deep. Then, she lays 30 eggs at one time. She quickly buries them so that they don't get eaten.

When the little Komodo dragons hatch, they dig out of the sand and run as fast as they can for the trees. Adult Komodo dragons are too big and heavy to climb trees. The baby Komodo dragons live in the trees for at least two years. The babies live on insects, birds, and bird eggs. They only climb down from the trees when they, too, are ready to be fierce hunters and fighters.

Komodo dragon: the largest of all known lizards
stubby: short and thick
prey: an animal taken for food

Living Large, Lizard Style

Imagine a lizard big enough to kill a buffalo. Science fiction? Not in Indonesia, where the Komodo dragon lives. This is a seriously large lizard—it can grow to be up to 10 feet (3.05 m) long and 200 pounds (90.72 kg). The Komodo dragon is so good at hunting that it is at the top of its food chain. That means no other animal can kill this huge "dragon." It has no predators.

The Komodo dragon has numerous **traits** that help it hunt. Even though it has short, stubby legs, it can run fast. If a Komodo dragon bites another animal, the **prey** will start to die. That's because the Komodo dragon has bacteria, or poisonous germs, in its mouth. After biting its prey, the Komodo dragon ambles slowly behind the animal until it drops to the ground.

This giant lizard also has a keen sense of smell. A Komodo dragon actually tastes the air with its forked tongue and can use its tongue to smell animals up to five miles (8.05 km) away. It has sharp claws and even sharper teeth. Its teeth have jagged edges and look like shark teeth. These teeth break off easily, but if they do, the Komodo dragon just grows more.

The Komodo dragon has an uncommon problem: it has no **scruples** and will eat its own kind. It will also eat another Komodo dragon's eggs. A mother has to scramble to hide her eggs. First, she gouges out a hole three feet (91.44 cm) deep. Then, she lays 30 eggs at one time. She quickly buries them so that they don't get eaten.

When the little Komodo dragons hatch, they dig out of the sand and run for the trees. Adult Komodo dragons are too big and hefty to climb trees. The baby Komodo dragons live in the trees for at least two years. They live on insects, birds, and bird eggs. They only **clamber** down when they are ready to be fierce hunters and fighters.

trait: a distinguishing characteristic
prey: an animal taken for prey
scruple: an ethical principle
clamber: climb

Name _____

Living Large, Lizard Style

Answer the questions.

1. What do you think it means for an animal to be *at the top of its food chain*?

   A. eaten by every other animal   **B.** no enemies; the strongest animal
   C. not enough food to eat   **D.** no food of the type the animal likes to eat

2. A Komodo dragon can be

   A. 20 feet (6.096 m) long and 200 (90.72 kg) pounds.
   B. 10 feet (3.05 m) long and 100 (45.36 kg) pounds.
   C. 10 feet (3.05 m) long and 400 (181.44 kg) pounds.
   D. 10 feet (3.05 m) long and 200 pounds (90.72 kg)

3. Look at the chain of events and answer the question.

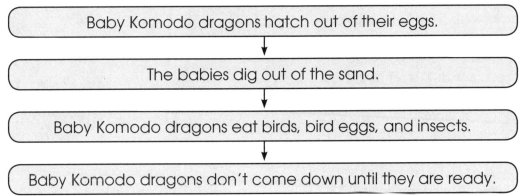

   Baby Komodo dragons hatch out of their eggs.

   The babies dig out of the sand.

   Baby Komodo dragons eat birds, bird eggs, and insects.

   Baby Komodo dragons don't come down until they are ready.

   Which step is missing?

   A. The baby Komodo dragons are led to burrows by their mothers.
   B. The baby Komodo dragons run to the trees.
   C. The baby Komodo dragons lie on the sand to warm up.
   D. The baby Komodo dragons dig burrows for themselves.

Match each adjective to the part of the Komodo dragon's body that it describes.

4. _____ stubby   **A.** teeth

5. _____ jagged-edged   **B.** legs

6. _____ forked   **C.** claws

7. _____ sharp   **D.** tongue

8. What is the main idea of the passage? What details help you answer this question?

   _____

9. On a separate sheet of paper, write a short story about an imaginary Komodo dragon that becomes a vegetarian. Compare it with a meat-eating Komodo dragon.

4.RI.4, 4.RI.10, 4.RF.4, 4.L.4

Footprints in the Snow

In 1951, Eric Shipton climbed Mount Everest, the highest mountain in the world. He and his team were looking around when they saw a scary sight. There were giant footprints in the snow! It looked like huge bare feet had made them. Each footprint was about 13 inches (33 cm) long. Shipton and his climbers followed the tracks for about one mile (1.6 km). It was not the first time he had seen huge footprints like these on Mount Everest.

Eric Shipton was a famous **explorer**. His pictures of the giant footprints were seen around the world. One of his **guides**, Sen Tensing, said that he and others had once seen this animal. He said that it was a **yeti**, a wild man. This barefoot creature had reddish-brown fur on half of his body. The yeti was over five feet (1.52 m) tall. Shipton believed Tensing. The explorer said that he was sure the footprints were not made by a bear or a mountain ape.

Others are not so sure. Some think that the huge footprints were made by a bear. They think the bear lives in the mountains and often walks on two legs. But, Shipton and his men followed the tracks for one mile (1.61 km). Would a bear walk that far on two legs when it could run on four? Others say that Tensing saw a mountain ape. But, mountain apes have five toes. These footprints had only four. Some think that the footprints were made by a smaller animal. Then, the sun melted them so that they looked bigger. Shipton said that the footprints were fresh. Could the sun have had time to melt them? Or, did the explorers really find the footprints of a strange, wild man of the mountain?

explorer: a person who travels to find out about something
guide: a person who leads others on a journey
yeti: known today as the abominable snowman

Footprints in the Snow

In 1951, Eric Shipton was climbing Mount Everest, the highest mountain in the world. He and his team were exploring when they saw a scary sight. There were giant footprints in the snow! It looked like huge bare feet had made them. Each footprint was about 13 inches (33 cm) long. Shipton and his climbers followed the tracks for about one mile (1.6 km). He said later that it was not the first time he had seen huge footprints like these on Mount Everest.

Eric Shipton was a famous **explorer**. His pictures of the giant footprints created excitement all over the world. And, there was more to the story. A man named Sen Tensing was one of Shipton's **guides**. Tensing said that he and others had once seen the creature that had made the prints. He said that it was a **yeti**, a wild man. This barefoot creature had reddish-brown fur on half of his body. The yeti was over five feet (1.52 m) tall. Shipton had someone question Tensing about the event. Shipton said that he believed Tensing. The explorer also said that he was sure the footprints were not made by a bear or a mountain ape.

Others are not so sure. Some think that the huge footprints were made by a bear that lives in the mountains and often walks on two legs. But, Shipton and his men followed the tracks for one mile (1.61 km). Would a bear have walked that far on two legs when it could run on four? Others say that Tensing saw a mountain ape. But, mountain apes have five toes, and these footprints had only four. Some scientists think that the footprints were made by a smaller animal. Then, the sun melted them so that they looked bigger. Shipton said that the footprints were fresh. Could the sun have had time to melt them? Or, did the explorers really find the footprints of a strange, wild man of the mountain?

explorer: a person who travels to find out about something
guide: a person who leads others on a journey
yeti: known today as the abominable snowman

Footprints in the Snow

In 1951, master climber Eric Shipton was ascending Mount Everest, the highest mountain in the world. He and his team were exploring when they saw a bloodcurdling sight. There were giant footprints in the snow! Each footprint measured about 13 inches (33 cm) long. Shipton and his climbers followed the tracks for about one mile (1.6 km). He said later that it was not the first time he had seen mysterious footprints like these on Mount Everest. This time, though, he recorded the **evidence** with a camera.

Eric Shipton was a famous explorer. His incredible pictures of the **mammoth** footprints created excitement all over the world. And, there was more to the story. A man named Sen Tensing was one of Shipton's guides. Tensing said that he and others had once before caught a glimpse of the baffling creature that had made the prints. He described it as a yeti, a wild man. This barefoot creature had reddish-brown fur on half of his body. The yeti was over five feet (1.52 m) tall. Shipton had someone question Tensing further about the event. Shipton said that he believed Tensing. The explorer also said that he was certain the footprints were not made by a bear or a mountain ape.

Some others are not **convinced**. Some think that the huge footprints were made by a bear that often walks on two legs. But, Shipton and his men followed the tracks for one mile (1.61 km). Would a bear have walked that far on two legs when it could more easily have run on four? Others say that Tensing saw a mountain ape. But, mountain apes have five toes, and these footprints had only four. Some scientists think that the footprints were made by a smaller animal. Then, the sun melted them so that they looked bigger. Shipton said that the footprints were fresh. Could the sun have had time to melt them? Or, did the explorers really **chance upon** the footprints of a strange, wild man of the mountain?

evidence: something that shows that something exists
mammoth: very large or immense
convince: to cause someone to believe something
chance upon: find, discover

Footprints in the Snow

Answer the questions.

1. What is a *yeti*? Write your answer in a complete sentence.

_____

2. Tensing said the yeti he saw had all of the following features except

    A. reddish-brown fur.   **B.** bare feet.

    C. fur all over his body.   **D.** large feet.

Write **T** for true or **F** for false.

3. _____ Eric Shipton was an explorer in the 1950s.

4. _____ Shipton saw strange tracks in the snow on Mount Fuji.

5. _____ Sen Tensing was Shipton's personal chef.

6. _____ Some scientists think the footprints melted in the sun.

7. _____ Mountain apes have four toes on each foot.

8. Choose the phrase that best completes the following sentence:

Mount Everest is _____.

    A. in North America   **B.** the tallest mountain on Earth

    C. a mountain range in Asia   **D.** none of the above

9. The explorers followed the strange tracks in the snow for

    A. one yard.   **B.** one kilometer.

    C. 1,000 yards.   **D.** one mile.

10. Eric Shipton probably did not believe that the tracks were made by a bear because

    A. bears have three toes on each foot.   **B.** bears do not walk that far on two legs.

    C. bears do not have reddish-brown fur.   **D.** bears do not have large feet.

11. What is the main idea of the passage? What details help you answer this question?

_____

_____

12. On a separate sheet of paper, write about how it would feel to come face to face with a yeti. Be sure to use correct spelling, capitalization, and punctuation.

Monster in the Loch

People say that a **monster** lives in Loch Ness, a big lake in Scotland. It is dark in color. It has a small head and a long neck. It swims like a seal. It is as big as a bus. Some people say it looks like a dinosaur.

Is this monster real? Stories about it go way back. Early visitors heard about strange animals in the lake. A **carving** was found of a huge, swimming creature. Written records of the Loch Ness Monster go back to AD 565.

A road was made around one side of the lake about 80 years ago. Then, people started to see a huge, dark, diving animal. It made waves in the lake. A circus owner offered thousands of dollars to anyone who could catch the animal for him!

People who live nearby say that they often see the black, swimming animal. A few years ago, a man found what might be a big cave under the lake. Could this be the Loch Ness Monster's home?

A few pictures have been taken of the Loch Ness Monster. One shows a strange animal with a long neck and little head. Sixty years later, someone proved that this photo was a fake. Two men made a head. They put it on a toy submarine. They put the model in the lake. Then, they took the picture. Another time, huge footprints were found near the lake. It turned out that they had been made with a stuffed hippo's foot!

Do a few tricks mean that the monster is a fake? Scientists are working to find **proof** that this famous animal exists. Then, we will know if there really is a monster in the deep, blue loch.

monster: a strange or frightening imaginary creature
carving: a carved figure or object
proof: something that shows that something else is true

Monster in the Loch

People say that a giant, swimming **monster** lives in Loch Ness, a big lake in Scotland. It is said to be dark in color. It has a small head and a long neck. It swims like a seal but is as big as a bus. Some people say it looks like a dinosaur.

Is this monster real? We know that the stories about it are very old. Early visitors to Scotland heard about strange animals in the lake. They even found a **carving** of a huge, swimming creature. Written records of the Loch Ness Monster go back to AD 565.

A road was built around one side of the lake in the 1930s. For the first time, people could get close to the north side of Loch Ness. People started to see a huge, dark, diving animal. They saw the waves it made in the lake. A circus owner offered thousands of dollars to anyone who could catch the creature for him!

People who live near Loch Ness say that they often see the black, swimming animal. A few years ago, a man training for the Coast Guard found what might be a big, underwater cave. Could this be the place where the Loch Ness Monster and its family live?

Only a few pictures have been taken of the Loch Ness Monster. The most famous one shows a strange animal with a long neck and small head. Then, someone proved that this photograph was a trick. Two men made a model of the head. They put it on a toy submarine. They put the model in the lake. Then, they took the picture. This wasn't the only Loch Ness Monster trick. In 1933, huge footprints were found near the lake. It turned out that someone had made them with a stuffed hippo's foot!

Do a few tricks mean that the monster is a fake? Every year, dozens of people report that they have seen the famous animal. Scientists keep working to find **proof**. Then, we will know if there really is a monster in the deep, blue loch.

monster: a strange or frightening imaginary creature
carving: a carved figure or object
proof: something that shows that something else is true

Monster in the Loch

The Scottish word for "lake" is *loch*. Loch Ness in Scotland is one of the deepest lakes in the world. The lake is world famous but not because of its amazing depth. People say that a giant, swimming monster lives in the lake. It is **rumored** to be dark in color, with a tiny head and a long neck. Eyewitnesses say it swims like a seal but is as big as a bus. Some people insist it resembles a dinosaur.

Is this monster **legitimate** or is it a figment of many people's imaginations? When Roman soldiers first arrived in Scotland, they heard whispers of the mysterious animals in the lake. They even discovered a carved **replica** of a huge, swimming creature. Written records of the Loch Ness Monster date back to AD 565. But, reports soared in the 1930s when a road was constructed around one side of the lake. People began spotting a huge, dark, diving animal with regularity. They even saw waves created in the lake when it swam or dived. Great excitement swelled. An **ambitious** circus owner offered thousands of dollars to anyone who could catch the elusive creature for him!

People who live near Loch Ness claim that they see the black, swimming animal often. A few years ago, a man training for the Coast Guard found what might be a big, underwater cave. Could this be the place where the Loch Ness Monster and its family live?

A few photographs have caught an image of this beast. The most famous one shows a creature with a long neck and small head. Years later, someone proved that this photograph was a trick. Two men made a model of the head. They fastened it to a toy submarine. They submerged the model in the lake. Then, they snapped the picture. Another time, huge footprints were discovered near the lake. Someone had made them with a stuffed hippo's foot!

Do a few tricks mean that the monster is a fake? Every year, dozens of people report that they have spotted the famous animal. Scientists keep working to find proof. Then, we will know if there really is a monster in the deep, blue loch.

rumored: a story told but not proven to be true
legitimate: real or accepted
replica: a close copy
ambitious: with a strong desire to succeed or achieve a goal

4.RI.1, 4.RI.9, 4.W.1, 4.L.3, 4.L.5

Monster in the Loch

Answer the questions.

1. What is a *loch*?

   A. a monster   **B.** a sea   **C.** a stream   **D.** a lake

2. What kind of phrase is *as big as a bus*?

   A. a metaphor   **B.** personification   **C.** an idiom   **D.** a simile

3. Write three words or phrases that precisely describe the Loch Ness Monster.

   A. _____

   B. _____

   C. _____

4. Finish the following sentence to tell about the trick picture.

   Two men made a _____ of the head and put it on a

   _____.

5. Besides this picture, which other Loch Ness Monster trick is described in the story?

   A. People made a fake film of the animal swimming.
   B. Somebody yelled that he could see the monster in the lake.
   C. Somebody made fake animal footprints near the lake.
   D. Two men made a model of the Loch Ness Monster.

6. Read the following sentence from the story and answer the question.

   Do a few tricks mean that the monster is a fake?

   Which of the following phrases could replace *is a fake*?

   A. is real   **B.** isn't real   **C.** is the truth   **D.** is silly

7. Read the story "Footprints in the Snow" about the yeti. Compare the story of the yeti with the story of the Loch Ness Monster. How are the two stories alike? How are they different?

   _____

   _____

8. Find Scotland on a map. Write two sentences about its location.

   _____

   _____

9. Write three things that you think would prove the monster is real. Write your answers in complete sentences on a separate sheet of paper.

Where Is Amelia?

Amelia Earhart flew airplanes at a time when women didn't do such things. She was the first woman to fly across the Atlantic Ocean. She made many **daring** trips. In 1937, Amelia planned to fly around the world. Instead, she vanished.

Most of her trip went well. She and her copilot got to the Pacific Ocean. On July 2, 1937, they planned to fly to a tiny island. A ship was nearby. It was there to listen for Amelia's messages on the radio.

The day was supposed to be clear. It was not. The flight took longer than planned. Amelia sent a message to the ship. She said her plane was getting low on gas. Then, she said she could not see the island. By that time, the plane had very little gas left. Amelia said she would keep sending messages. After that, there was only silence.

The president of the United States called for a **search**. Over four million dollars was spent to try to find the lost pilot. Ships searched over 250,000 square miles (647,497 sq. km) of sea. The work lasted two weeks. No clues were found.

At first, people thought that the plane had just run out of gas. It must have crashed into the sea. Then, Amelia's mother told reporters that her daughter may have planned her trip for the government. Other people said Amelia was looking for facts about ships from Japan. Was Amelia Earhart a spy?

The search still goes on for Amelia Earhart. Many people have looked for her airplane.

One person thought he had found her grave, but he had not. Other people have found parts of planes. They thought the parts were from the crash of Amelia's airplane. But, many planes crashed in the Pacific Ocean during World War II.

No **proof** has ever been found that Amelia was a spy. Her body and her plane have never been found. We may never know the whole story about this great pilot. She is gone, but her story lives on.

daring: willing to do dangerous things
search: an attempt to find something
proof: something that shows that something else is true or real

Where Is Amelia?

Amelia Earhart flew airplanes at a time when women rarely did such things. She made many **daring** trips and was the first woman to fly across the Atlantic Ocean. In 1937, Amelia planned to fly around the world. Instead, she **vanished**.

Most of her trip went well. She and her copilot made it to the Pacific Ocean. On July 2, 1937, they planned to fly to a tiny island. This would be the toughest leg of their trip. A ship waited nearby. Its mission was to listen for Amelia's messages on the radio.

The day was supposed to be clear, but it wasn't. The flight took longer than planned. Amelia sent a message to say that her plane was getting low on gas. Her last static-filled message said she could not see the island. By that time, the plane had very little gas left. Amelia was never heard from again.

The president of the United States called for a **search**. Over four million dollars was spent to try to find the lost pilot. Ships searched over 250,000 square miles (647,497 sq. km) of sea. The work lasted two weeks. No clues were ever found.

At first, people thought that the plane had just run out of gas. It must have crashed into the sea and sunk too low to be found. Then, Amelia's mother told reporters that her daughter may have planned her trip for the government. Other people said Amelia was looking for facts about Japanese ships. Was Amelia Earhart a spy?

The search still goes on for Amelia Earhart. Many people have looked for her airplane.

One person thought he had found her grave, but he had not. Other people have found parts of planes. They thought the parts were from the crash of Amelia's airplane. But, many planes crashed in the Pacific Ocean during World War II.

No **proof** has ever been found that Amelia was a spy. Her body and her plane have never been found. We may never know the whole story about this great pilot. She is gone, but her story lives on.

daring: willing to do dangerous things
vanish: to disappear
search: an attempt to find something
proof: something that shows that something else is true or real

Where Is Amelia?

Amelia Earhart set many flying records at a time when women didn't do things like that. She made many daring trips and was the first woman to fly solo across both the Atlantic and Pacific Oceans. In 1937, Amelia planned to fly around the world. Instead, she **vanished**.

Most of her trip went well. She and her copilot got to the Pacific Ocean. On July 2, 1937, they planned to fly to a tiny island. A ship was **anchored** nearby to listen for Amelia's radio message.

The day was supposed to be clear, but instead, it was cloudy. The flight took longer than originally planned. Amelia sent a message to the ship. She said her plane was getting low on gas. Then, she said **visibility** was poor and she could not see the island. By that time, the plane had very little gas left. Amelia said she would keep sending messages. Then, there was only silence.

The president of the United States called for a search. Over four million dollars was spent to try to find the lost pilot. Ships searched over 250,000 square miles (647,497 sq. km) of sea. The search lasted two weeks. No clues were found concerning Amelia or her plane.

At first, people thought that the plane had just run out of gas and crashed into the sea. Then, Amelia's mother told a reporter about her **suspicions** that her daughter may have been working for the government. Rumors questioned if Amelia Earhart was a spy looking for facts about Japanese ships.

The search still goes on for Amelia Earhart. Many people have looked for her airplane.

One person wrongly thought he had found her grave. Other people have found parts of planes they thought were from the crash of Amelia's airplane. But, many planes crashed in the Pacific Ocean during World War II.

No proof has been found that Amelia was a spy. Her body and her plane have never been found. Her disappearance is one of the most enduring mysteries of the 21st century.

vanish: to disappear
anchor: to keep a ship from moving
visibility: the ability to be seen
suspicion: a feeling that something is true, usually something bad

Where Is Amelia?

Answer the questions.

1. Which of the following is a synonym for *vanished*?

    A. valued   **B.** disappeared

    C. ventured   **D.** revisited

2. According to the story, what was one cause of Amelia's flight problems on July 2?

    A. She and her copilot were fighting.   **B.** The radio didn't work on the plane.

    C. The island wasn't on the map.   **D.** The weather was bad.

3. What is one adjective that describes Amelia Earhart? _____

4. Which of the following sentences best summarizes the story?

    A. There have been many theories about what happened to Amelia Earhart.

    B. It has been proven that Amelia Earhart was arrested by the Japanese.

    C. Amelia Earhart was a famous pilot, but no one really searches for her anymore.

    D. Amelia Earhart was on a flight to spy for the president.

5. Why would the president of the United States want to know more about Japanese ships?

    A. He really liked ships.

    B. He wanted to build ships like the Japanese ships.

    C. The United States fought against the ships during World War II.

    D. He knew that Amelia Earhart liked ships.

6. What is a spy?

    A. an adviser to the president

    B. someone who looks for secrets from another government

    C. someone who goes on flights around the world

    D. none of the above

7. Which is the best reason to think that Amelia Earhart might have been a spy?

    A. A movie hinted about it.

    B. The Japanese arrested Amelia.

    C. Her mother said Amelia may have been working for the government.

    D. Her plane was filled with secret information that she had found on her trip.

8. How did the events of World War II affect the story of Amelia Earhart?

_____

9. What do you think happened to Amelia Earhart? Write your opinion on a separate sheet of paper. Ask a classmate or a teacher to edit your writing. Then, revise your work.

Fly Me to the Moon

Would you like to fly into space? In the past, only astronauts could do that. Someday soon, people may be able to take vacations in space! That's the hope of the crew working on *SpaceShipOne*.

SpaceShipOne is like an airplane with a rocket engine. The special engine gives the **spacecraft thrust**, which is a big lift up. A large airplane, called the *White Knight*, carries *SpaceShipOne* into the air. When the *White Knight* lets *SpaceShipOne* go, the spacecraft's engine mixes a special type of gas with rubber. This mixture causes a reaction that sends the spaceship high enough to go into **orbit**.

People working on *SpaceShipOne* have to fix some problems. When it first takes off, the thrust can make it roll in the air. Keeping the spacecraft on the right course is also hard. The higher it goes, the stronger the wind. The wind blows the spaceship off course. But, workers feel that soon these problems will be fixed.

What will spacecrafts like *SpaceShipOne* be used for? For now, they will just make trips into space. People will pay thousands of dollars to fly high enough to see the stars. One day, there may even be hotels that orbit the earth. Space stations could have rooms where tourists can stay. Imagine spending a vacation in a room in space!

Maybe someday spacecrafts like these will travel to other planets. People may build towns there. They will need to go back and forth to visit Earth. Spacecrafts like *SpaceShipOne* could play a part in those plans.

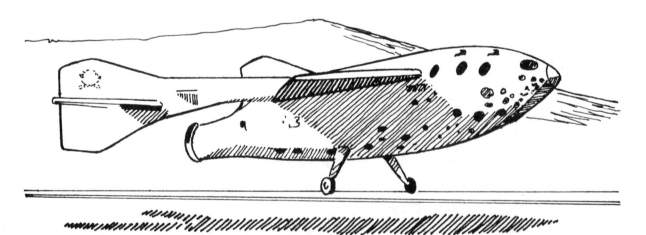

spacecraft: a vehicle designed for travel in outer space
thrust: a strong forward or upward movement
orbit: a circular path, usually of one body around another body

Fly Me to the Moon

Would you like to fly into space? In the past, only astronauts were able to do that. Governments chose the people who went into space. Someday soon, though, people may be able to take vacations in space! That's the hope of the crew working on *SpaceShipOne*.

SpaceShipOne is like an airplane with a rocket engine. The special engine gives the **spacecraft thrust**, which is a big boost upward. A large airplane, called the *White Knight*, carries *SpaceShipOne* into the air. When the *White Knight* releases *SpaceShipOne*, the spacecraft's engine mixes a special type of gas with rubber. This chemical mixture causes a reaction that sends the spaceship high enough to go into **orbit**.

The people working on *SpaceShipOne* have to fix some problems. When it first takes off, the thrust can make it roll in the air. Keeping the spacecraft on course is also difficult. The higher it goes, the stronger the force of the wind. The wind blows the spaceship off course. But, workers feel that soon these problems will be resolved.

What is the purpose of spacecrafts like *SpaceShipOne*? For now, they will just make trips into space. People will pay thousands of dollars to fly high enough to see the stars. One day, there may even be hotels that orbit the earth. Space stations could have rooms where tourists can stay. Imagine spending a vacation in a room in space. Think about the view!

Maybe someday spacecrafts like these will travel to other planets. People may construct colonies there. They will need to go back and forth to visit Earth for supplies or to visit friends and relatives. Spacecrafts like *SpaceShipOne* could play a part in those plans.

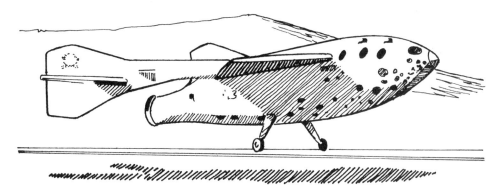

spacecraft: a vehicle designed for travel in outer space
thrust: a strong forward or upward movement
orbit: a circular path, usually of one body around another body

Fly Me to the Moon

Have you ever dreamed of flying into outer space? **Historically**, only astronauts were involved in space travel. Governments chose who could travel into space. But someday soon, anyone may be able to take vacations in space! That's the sincere hope of the crew working on *SpaceShipOne*, the first nongovernment manned spacecraft.

SpaceShipOne is much like an airplane, but it is powered by a rocket engine. The special engine gives the spacecraft thrust, which is a big boost upward. A large **turbojet**, called the *White Knight*, carries *SpaceShipOne* into the air attached to its underbelly. When the *White Knight* releases *SpaceShipOne*, the spacecraft's engine mixes a special type of gas with rubber. This chemical mixture is called a propellant. It causes a chemical reaction that propels the spaceship high enough to go into orbit.

People working on *SpaceShipOne* have to fix some problems. When it first takes off, the thrust can make it roll in the air. Keeping the spacecraft on course is also hard. The higher it goes, the stronger the force of the wind. The wind blows the spaceship off course. But, workers feel that soon these problems will be **eliminated**.

What will be the purpose of spacecrafts like *SpaceShipOne*? For now, they will simply make trips into space. People will pay thousands of dollars to fly high enough to see the stars. One day, there may even be hotels that orbit the earth. Space tourism may become a common vacation option. Space stations may have rooms where tourists can stay. Imagine spending a vacation in a room in space. Consider the great view you would have!

There is a great **potential** for spacecrafts like these to travel someday to other planets. People may construct colonies there. They will need to go back and forth to Earth for supplies or to visit friends and relatives. Spacecrafts like *SpaceShipOne* could play an essential part in those plans.

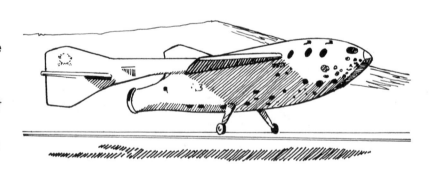

historically: in the past
turbojet: an airplane with powerful turbojet engines
eliminate: to get rid of
potential: having possibility

Name _____

4.RI.2, 4.RI.4, 4.RI.5, 4.W.1, 4.W.6

Fly Me to the Moon

Answer the questions.

1. Read the following sentence from the story and answer the question.

   The wind blows the spaceship off course.

   What does *off course* mean?

   A. away from Earth

   B. off the path it is supposed to travel

   C. off the map so that it cannot be charted

   D. away from space

2. Which sentence best summarizes the main idea of the story?

   A. Private spacecrafts with rocket engines are not perfect yet.

   B. Private spacecrafts are better than rockets for travel.

   C. Space stations may someday be used as hotels.

   D. Space travel may soon be possible for many people, not just astronauts.

3. Which of the following sentences is an opinion?

   A. Maybe someday spacecrafts like these will travel to other planets.

   B. *SpaceShipOne* is like an airplane with a rocket engine.

   C. Governments chose the people who went into space.

   D. When *SpaceShipOne* first takes off, the thrust can make it roll in the air.

4. What is the meaning of *thrust* as it is used in this story?

   A. a big boost upward

   B. to push into someone's hands

   C. the main point of something

   D. none of the above

5. *SpaceShipOne* is flown into the air by a big airplane called _____.

6. Tourists may someday have rooms in a _____.

7. *SpaceShipOne*'s thrust is created by mixing _____ with rubber.

8. Name two possible problems connected with taking people into outer space.

   _____   _____

9. Name two possible solutions to the problems you listed in question 8.

   _____   _____

10. Do you think that people will live in colonies on other planets someday? Why or why not? Write your answer in complete sentences on a separate sheet of paper. Revise and edit your piece. Then, type it on a computer. Share your finished work with a classmate or teacher.

The Machines That Found the *Titanic*

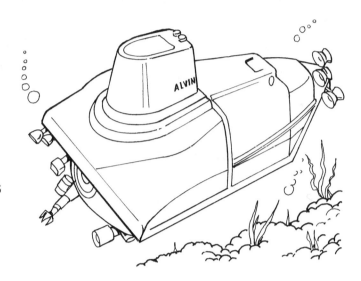

The great ship *Titanic* sank in 1912. For over 70 years, no one could find it. It was lost on the ocean floor. Then, an explorer named Dr. Robert Ballard looked for the *Titanic*. He used three special machines.

Dr. Ballard **invented** a machine called Argo. Argo is like a big sled. It was pulled below Dr. Ballard's ship. It uses **sonar** to look at the ocean floor. Argo took pictures and sent them back to Dr. Ballard's ship. On September 1, 1985, Argo found a big part of the *Titanic*. The great ship was found!

Dr. Ballard was ready to go down to look at the *Titanic*. He used another special machine called *Alvin*. *Alvin* is a small, round submarine that holds three people. It was built to work in very deep water. The *Titanic* was 12,000 feet (3,657.6 m) under the water. It took Dr. Ballard and two other **crew** members 2.5 hours just to go down that far! Unlike other submarines, *Alvin* can land on the sea floor. It has special lights to help the explorers see. And, it holds another machine for more help.

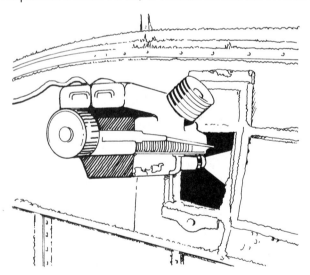

The third machine was called *Jason Junior*. The crew called it "JJ" for short. JJ is a little, floating robot. JJ rides inside *Alvin* in a space called "the garage." When Dr. Ballard opened the garage doors, JJ floated out in front of *Alvin*. The robot is linked to *Alvin* by a 300-foot (91.44 m) cable. Dr. Ballard and other crew members could make JJ move any way that they wanted. JJ was small enough to go into the ship. It sent back pictures that Dr. Ballard could study.

invent: to think of something for the first time
sonar: a device that uses sound waves to find things that are underwater
crew: a group of people who work on the same project together

The Machines That Found the *Titanic*

The great ship *Titanic* sank in 1912. For over 70 years, no one could find its **wreckage** on the ocean floor. Then, an explorer named Dr. Robert Ballard decided to search for the *Titanic*. He used three special machines that helped him make history.

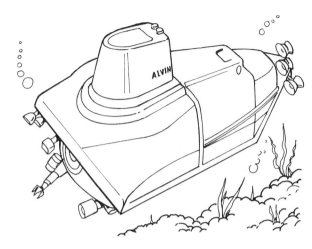

The first machine was one that Dr. Ballard invented. It is called Argo. Argo is like a big sled. It was towed underwater below Dr. Ballard's ship. It uses **sonar** to scan the ocean floor by bouncing sound off of it. If the sound waves bounce off a shape, that shape shows on a screen. Argo sent pictures back to Dr. Ballard's ship. On September 1, 1985, Argo found something big in a trail of **debris**. It was a boiler from the engine of the *Titanic*. The great ship was found!

Dr. Ballard was ready to go down to look at the *Titanic*. He used another special machine called *Alvin*. *Alvin* is a small, round submarine that holds three people. It was built to work in very deep water. The *Titanic* was 12,000 feet (3657.6 m) under the water. It took Dr. Ballard and two other crew members 2.5 hours just to go that deep into the sea! Unlike other submarines, *Alvin* can land on the sea floor. It has special lights to help the explorers see. And, it holds another machine for more help.

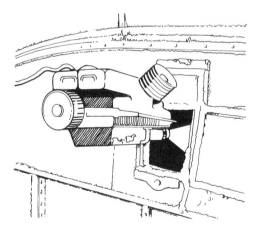

The third machine used to help explore the *Titanic* was called *Jason Junior*. The crew called it "JJ" for short. JJ is a small, floating robot. JJ rides inside *Alvin* in a space called "the garage." When Dr. Ballard opened the garage doors, JJ floated out in front of *Alvin*. The robot is linked to *Alvin* by a 300-foot (91.44 m) cable. Dr. Ballard and other crew members could make JJ move any way that they wanted. The *Titanic* wreck is too deep and unsafe for divers to explore. But, JJ was small enough to go into the ship. It sent back pictures for the explorers to study.

wreckage: the broken parts of something that has been damaged
sonar: a device that uses sound waves to find things that are underwater
debris: pieces left over after something has been destroyed

The Machines That Found the *Titanic*

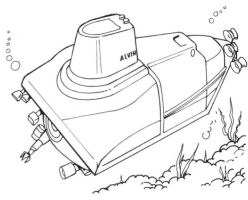

The great ship *Titanic* sank in 1912. For over 70 years, no one could find its **wreckage** on the ocean floor. Then, an explorer and **oceanographer** named Dr. Robert Ballard decided to search for the *Titanic*. He used three special machines that helped him make history.

The first machine was one that Dr. Ballard invented. It is called Argo. Argo is like a big sled. It was towed underwater below Dr. Ballard's ship. It uses sonar to scan the ocean floor by bouncing sound off of it. If the sound waves bounce off of a shape, that shape shows on a screen. Argo sent pictures back to Dr. Ballard's ship. On September 1, 1985, Argo found something big in a trail of **debris**. It was a boiler from the engine of the *Titanic*. The great ship was found!

Dr. Ballard was ready to go down to look at the *Titanic*. He used another special machine called *Alvin. Alvin* is a small, round submarine that holds three people. It was built to operate in very deep water. The *Titanic* was 12,000 feet (3657.6 m) under the water. It took Dr. Ballard and two other crew members 2.5 hours just to go that deep into the sea! Unlike other submarines, *Alvin* can land on the sea floor. It has special lights to help the explorers see. And, it holds another machine for more help.

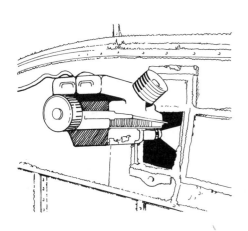

The third machine used to help explore the *Titanic* was called *Jason Junior*. The crew called it "JJ" for short. JJ is a small, floating robot on a leash, linked to *Alvin* by a 300-foot (91.44 m) cable. JJ rides inside *Alvin* in a compartment called "the garage." When Dr. Ballard opened the garage doors, JJ floated out ahead of *Alvin*. Dr. Ballard and other crew members could **manipulate** JJ to move any way that they wanted. The *Titanic* wreckage is too deep and unsafe for human divers to explore, so JJ was a perfect substitute. JJ was small enough to go into the ship and send back pictures that the explorers were able to study.

---

wreckage: the broken parts of something that has been damaged
oceanographer: a scientist who studies oceans
debris: pieces left over after something has been destroyed
manipulate: to move or control something

Name _____

The Machines That Found the *Titanic*

Answer the questions.

1. What is an antonym for *special*?

   A. interesting   **B.** unusual   **C.** ordinary   **D.** different

2. How did the explorers first know they had found the *Titanic*?

   A. *Alvin* sent them pictures of the ship.
   B. They went to the floor of the sea and saw the wreck.
   C. They had a map that showed them where the ship was.
   D. *Argo* sent them pictures of part of the *Titanic*'s engine.

3. Describe Argo. Write your answer in complete sentences.

   _____

   _____

4. Why did the explorers need JJ?

   A. It was not safe for them to dive and go into the *Titanic* themselves.
   B. JJ was small enough to fit inside the ship.
   C. They wanted to see inside the ship, and JJ had cameras to take pictures.
   D. all of the above

5. Why do you think *Alvin* could not go inside the *Titanic*?

   A. *Alvin* was too big.   **B.** *Alvin* could not be controlled.
   C. *Alvin* could not go up and down.   **D.** *Alvin* would not be able to get out.

6. Which of the following is an opinion?

   A. *Argo* uses both sonar and cameras.
   B. *Alvin* was built to work in the deep sea.
   C. Finding the *Titanic* was the most important discovery ever.
   D. Dr. Ballard invented Argo.

7. Which of the following is not true?

   A. The *Titanic* was found at a depth of 12,000 feet (3,657.6 m).
   B. Other ships used sonar to look for the *Titanic* in the past.
   C. JJ took pictures inside cabins on the ship.
   D. Dr. Ballard was the first person to look for the wreck of the *Titanic*.

8. On a separate sheet of paper, describe the kinds of things you might find if you could explore inside the wrecked ship's dining room, kitchen, or a guest cabin. Use the Internet, books, or magazines for additional information. Include a drawing of the room you choose.

Behind the Bookcase

Anne Frank was only four when her father moved his family from Germany to Holland. They ran away because they were Jews. The **Nazis** were taking over. Otto Frank knew that the Jews in Germany were in danger.

Anne liked her new life in Holland. She made new friends. She went to school. But then, World War II started. The Nazis took over Holland. Otto Frank had to find another safe place to hide his family. He owned a building with offices and workrooms. He built a **secret** place behind a bookcase in one of the offices. The bookcase moved away from the wall. It was the door to the hiding place. The Frank family and another family moved there in 1942. Anne took her new birthday present with her. It was a blank **diary**. She wrote in her diary every day.

Two long years passed. The families lived in their secret place. They could not walk or move during the day. The workers below might hear them. They could only talk, cook, and walk at night. They never went outside. They were very careful. But, the Nazis still found them. They were arrested in 1944. They were taken to a camp. Only Otto Frank lived to see the end of the war.

Something else **survived**, too. Anne's diary was still behind the bookcase in the secret rooms. It told the story of their life in hiding. Anne was only 13 years old when she started it. The diary showed that she was a good writer. Her father thought other people should read Anne's diary. The book was printed and came out in 1949. This moving story about their lives is still read today.

Nazis: members of a political party in Germany from 1933 to 1945
secret: hidden from view
diary: a book with daily notes about one's life or thoughts
survive: to stay alive

Behind the Bookcase

When Anne Frank was only four years old, her father decided that he had to move his family from Germany to Holland. They ran away because they were Jews. The **Nazis** were taking over. Otto Frank knew that the Jews in Germany were in danger.

Anne liked her new life in Holland. She made new friends. She went to school. But then, World War II started. The Nazis took over Holland. Otto Frank had to find another safe place to hide his family. He owned a building with offices and workrooms. He built a secret place behind a bookcase in one of the offices. The bookcase moved away from the wall. It was the door to the hiding place. The Frank family and another family moved there in 1942. Anne took her new birthday present with her. It was a blank **diary**. She wrote in her diary every day.

Two long years passed. The families lived in their secret place. They could not walk or move during the day. The workers below might hear them. They could only talk, cook, and walk at night. They never went outside. They were very careful. But, the Nazis still found them. They were arrested in 1944. They were taken to a prison camp. Only Otto Frank lived to see the end of the war.

Something else **survived**, too. Anne's diary was still behind the bookcase in the secret rooms. It told the story of their life in hiding. Anne was only 13 years old when she started it. The diary showed that she was a fine writer. All of the things she hoped for and feared were written down. Her father thought other people should read Anne's diary. The book was printed and **released** in 1949. This moving story about the lives of two Jewish families during World War II is still read today. In it, Anne's amazing spirit is still alive.

Nazis: members of a political party in Germany from 1933 to 1945
diary: a book with daily notes about one's life or thoughts
survive: to stay alive
release: to put out into the public

4.RI.4, 4.RI.10, 4.RF.4, 4.L.4

Behind the Bookcase

Anne Frank was only four years old when an unbelievable nightmare started for her family. Her father decided that he had to **relocate** his family from Germany to Holland. They fled because they were Jews. The **Nazis** were taking power. Otto Frank knew that the Jews in Germany were in danger.

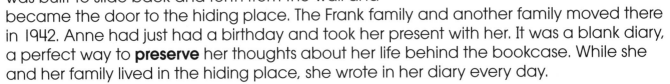

Anne liked her new life in Holland. She made new friends and enjoyed her new school. But then, World War II started. The Nazis took over Holland, and the nightmare began all over again. Otto Frank had to find a safe place to hide his family. Luckily, he owned a building with offices and workrooms. He quickly constructed a secret hiding place behind a bookcase in one of the offices. The bookcase was built to slide back and forth from the wall and became the door to the hiding place. The Frank family and another family moved there in 1942. Anne had just had a birthday and took her present with her. It was a blank diary, a perfect way to **preserve** her thoughts about her life behind the bookcase. While she and her family lived in the hiding place, she wrote in her diary every day.

Two long, desperate years passed. The families remained **holed up** in their secret place. They could not walk or move during the day for fear the workers below might hear them. They could only talk, cook, and walk at night when the building was empty. They never went outside. They were very careful, but the Nazis still found them. They were arrested in 1944 and taken to a prison camp. Only Otto Frank lived to see the end of the war.

Something else survived, too. Anne's diary remained intact behind the bookcase in the secret rooms. It told the story of her life in hiding. Even though she was only 13 years old when she started it, Anne's diary showed that she was a fine writer. All of the things she hoped for and feared were written down. Her father thought other people should read Anne's diary. The book was printed and released in 1949. This moving story about the lives of two Jewish families during World War II is still read today. In it, Anne's amazing spirit is still alive.

---

relocate: move to another place
Nazis: members of a political party in Germany from 1933 to 1945
preserve: to keep safe
hole up: to hide as if in a hole

Behind the Bookcase

Answer the questions.

1. Read the following sentence and answer the question.

   This moving story is still read today.

   Which of the following definitions of the word *moving* is used in the sentence?

   A. traveling from one place to another   **B.** carrying furniture to a new place

   C. a kind of ticket for a car accident   **D.** deeply touching

2. Why did Anne and her family have to go into hiding? Write your answer in a complete sentence.

   _____

   _____

3. Which of these is not a feature of the Frank family's hiding place?

   A. had a door so that they could   **B.** had a doorway hidden behind
   go outside at night   a bookcase

   C. housed two families   **D.** was in an office building

Write **T** for true or **F** for false.

4. _____ Anne was two years old when her family left Germany.

5. _____ The Nazis took over Holland after World War II started.

6. _____ Anne wrote about their hiding place on a computer.

7. _____ Two families hid in the secret rooms in the office building.

8. _____ Otto Frank had Anne's diary published after the war ended.

9. List five of the main events of the Frank family's story in order.

   A. _____

   B. _____

   C. _____

   D. _____

   E. _____

10. On a separate sheet of paper, write about what you would do (and why) if you had to hide quietly for a whole day. Link your ideas and reasons with words like *another, for example, also,* and *because.*

The Gravity of Childhood

Sir Isaac Newton was the first person to be able to explain **gravity**. He was a very important scientist and thinker. But, the start of his life was hard. He overcame many troubles to become successful later in his life.

Isaac was born on Christmas Day in 1642. His father had just died. When Isaac was three years old, his mother married again. Her new husband did not want Isaac. So, the little boy was raised by his grandmother.

When Isaac started school, he was far behind the other boys in his class. He was second from the last in his grade! Things did not look good for Isaac Newton. But, he was a good learner. He also spent much of his time outside. He flew kites and watched how the wind moved them. He watched the clouds and the stars. He carved models and played with them. Once, he made a little windmill. It was **powered** by a mouse running on a treadmill. He was always busy. He was always thinking.

All of his work **paid off**. By the time Isaac left school, he was first in his class. All of the time he spent watching the world paid off too. One day, Isaac was sitting at home and looking out a window. He saw an apple fall from a tree. Suddenly, he wondered why apples always fall to the ground. Why don't they fall up to the sky? Why don't they fall sideways? Each apple always falls toward the center of the earth.

That was when Isaac first started thinking about gravity, the force that pulls things toward the earth. It was only one of his important ideas. He also worked math problems. He was the first person who thought about gravity and the orbit of the moon. He also wrote about color and light. Isaac Newton had many of his famous ideas during his lonely but thoughtful childhood.

gravity: a natural force that causes things to fall toward the earth
powered: gave force to
paid off: gave positive results

The Gravity of Childhood

Sir Isaac Newton was the first person to be able to explain **gravity**. He was a very important scientist and thinker. But, his life had a rough start. He overcame many misfortunes to become successful later in his life.

Isaac was born on Christmas Day in 1642. His father had just died. When Isaac was three years old, his mother married again. Her new husband did not want Isaac. So, the little boy was raised by his grandmother.

When Isaac started school, he was far behind the other boys in his class. He was second from the last in his grade! Things did not look good for Isaac Newton, but he was a good student. He also spent much of his time outside. He flew kites and watched how the wind moved them. He observed the clouds and the stars. He carved models and played with them. Once, he made a little windmill that was **powered** by a mouse running on a treadmill. He was always busy, always thinking.

The hard work **paid off**. By the time Isaac left school, he was first in his class. All of the time he spent watching the natural world paid off too. One day, Isaac was sitting at home. He looked out a window and saw an apple fall from a tree. Suddenly, he wondered why apples always fall to the ground. Why don't they ever fall up to the sky? Why don't they ever fall sideways? An apple always falls toward the center of the earth.

That was when Isaac first started thinking about gravity, the force that pulls things toward the earth. It was only one of his important ideas. He also worked math problems. He was the first person who thought about gravity and how it related to the orbit of the moon. He also wrote about color and light. Isaac Newton had many of his famous ideas during his lonely but thoughtful childhood.

gravity: a natural force that causes things to fall toward the earth
powered: gave force to
paid off: gave positive results

The Gravity of Childhood

Sir Isaac Newton was the first person to be able to explain the laws, or principles, of **gravity**. Isaac had a brilliant mind and became a well-known scientist and **philosopher**. But, his life had a rough start. He had to overcome many misfortunes to become successful later in his life.

Isaac was born on Christmas Day in 1642. His father, a **prosperous** farmer, had just died three months earlier. Isaac was named after him. When Isaac was three years old, his mother married again. Her new husband, a local minister, did not want Isaac. So, the little boy was raised by his grandmother.

When Isaac started school, he was far behind the other boys in his class. In fact, he was second from the last in his grade! Isaac Newton's future did not look bright, but he was a **diligent** student. He also spent much of his time outdoors. He flew kites and watched how the wind flipped and tugged at them. He observed the clouds and the stars. He carved models and played with them. Once, he made a little windmill that was powered by a mouse running on a treadmill. He was always busy, always thinking.

The hard work paid off. By the time Isaac left school, he was first in his class. All of the time he spent watching the natural world paid off, too. One day, while sitting by a window at home, Isaac saw an apple fall from a tree. Suddenly, he was curious about why apples always fall to the ground. Why don't they ever fall up to the sky? Why don't they ever fall sideways? He knew that an apple always falls toward the center of the earth.

His curiosity got the best of him. Isaac first started thinking about gravity, the force that pulls things toward the earth. His theory of gravity is well known, but it was only one of his important ideas. He also worked complicated math problems. He was the first person who considered gravity and how it related to the orbit of the moon. He also wrote about color and light. Many of Isaac Newton's famous ideas occurred to him during his lonely but thoughtful childhood.

gravity: a natural force that causes things to fall toward the earth
philosopher: a person who studies ideas
prosperous: wealthy
diligent: steady, hardworking

The Gravity of Childhood

Answer the questions.

1. _____ is the force that pulls things toward the earth.

2. Sir Isaac Newton was born on _____ in the year
_____.

3. Even though he was not a good student at first, Isaac Newton was a good
_____.

4. In order to study the wind, Isaac flew _____.

5. Isaac Newton lived with his _____ after he was three years
old.

Write **T** for true or **F** for false.

6. _____ One of Isaac Newton's ideas was about how gravity affects the moon's
orbit.

7. _____ Isaac first thought about gravity when he saw a squirrel jump out of a tree.

8. _____ Isaac built a little model of an airplane.

9. _____ Another idea that Isaac explored was about color and light.

10. Read the following sentence and answer the question.

All of his work paid off.

Which phrase could replace *paid off* in the sentence?

   A. made him poor   **B.** made him successful

   C. made him tired   **D.** paid his bills

11. Write at least five compound words found in the passage.

_____

_____

12. In your opinion, what was Isaac Newton's most important idea? Why do you
think so? Write your answer in complete sentences on a separate sheet of paper.
Remember to state your opinion, list your reasons, and write a concluding sentence.

A Mind for New Ideas

Thomas Edison did not go to school for very long. He had too many questions. After only 12 weeks, his teacher gave up. So, Thomas's mother taught him at home.

Thomas got a job in 1859 when he was only 12 years old. He sold newspapers, candy, and fruit on a train. He kept a little room on one of the cars of the train. He played around with the **telegraph**, an exciting new machine. Thomas went to work in a telegraph office when he was older. He loved electricity and what it could do.

Thomas received his first patent for an invention when he was 21. A patent is a notice from the government. The patent said that Thomas owned his idea. Other people could not copy it. His invention was a voting machine. Then, he worked hard on other inventions. In 1877, he invented the **phonograph**. It played voices and music. Two years later, he invented something even more important. It was a lightbulb. Thomas also worked to give lighting to homes, streets, and stores.

Soon, Thomas had more than 200 people working for him. He still had lots of ideas. He improved his phonograph. He invented the **battery** and the first movie camera. Thomas only cared about ideas that helped people. And, he wanted to make things that people could easily pay for.

Thomas Edison created more ideas and inventions than any other inventor. He dreamed of a world of light, sound, and movement, and then he made it real.

telegraph: a device for sending messages by radio signals
phonograph: an instrument that used a needle on a record to produce sounds
battery: two or more cells that together produce electricity

A Mind for New Ideas

Thomas Edison did not stay in school very long. He asked too many questions. After only 12 weeks, his teacher was tired. So, Thomas's mother taught him at home.

Thomas got a job in 1859 when he was only 12 years old. He sold newspapers, candy, and fruit on a train. He built a little lab for himself in one of the cars of the train. He did experiments with the **telegraph**, an exciting new machine. Thomas went to work in a telegraph office when he was older. He loved electricity and what it could do.

Thomas received his first patent for an invention at the age of 21. A patent is a notice from the government. The patent said that Thomas owned his idea and that other people could not copy it. His invention was a voting machine. Then, he started working hard on other inventions. In 1877, he invented something that amazed the world: a **phonograph**. It played voices and music. Two years later, he invented something even more important. It was a lightbulb. Thomas also worked to bring lighting to homes, streets, and stores.

Soon, Thomas had more than 200 people working for him. He still had lots of ideas. He improved his phonograph. He invented the **battery** and the first movie camera. Thomas was not interested in ideas that did not help people. And, he did not want to make things that people could not pay for.

Thomas Edison created more ideas and inventions for the modern world than any other inventor. He dreamed of a world of light, sound, and movement, and then he made it real.

telegraph: a device for sending messages by radio signals
phonograph: an instrument that used a needle on a record to produce sounds
battery: two or more cells that together produce electricity

A Mind for New Ideas

Thomas Edison did not stay in school very long. He had too many questions. He wanted to know too much. After only 12 weeks, his teacher was **exhausted**. So, Thomas's mother taught him at home instead. Later, Thomas said that his mother "was the making of me."

Thomas started working in 1859 when he was 12 years old. He sold newspapers, candy, and fruit on a train. He built a little lab for himself in one of the cars of the train. He did experiments with the **telegraph**, an exciting new machine. Thomas went to work in a telegraph office when he was older. He loved electricity and what it could do.

Thomas received his first patent for an invention at the age of 21. A patent is a notice from the government. The patent said that Thomas owned his idea and that other people could not copy it. His invention was a voting machine. After receiving his patent, he started working hard on other inventions. In 1877, he invented something that amazed the world: a **phonograph**. It recorded and played voices and music. Two years later, he invented something even more important. It was a lightbulb. Thomas also worked to create power **systems** so that homes, streets, and stores could have lighting.

Thomas built a group of lab buildings in New Jersey. More than 200 people worked for him. He had many different ideas. For years, Thomas worked on one idea after another. He improved his phonograph. He invented the battery. He made the first movie camera. Thomas always wanted his inventions to work for people. He was not interested in ideas that did not help people. And, he did not want to make things that people could not afford. Thomas Edison is responsible for more ideas and inventions for the modern world than any other inventor. He dreamed of a world of light, sound, and movement, and then he made it real.

exhausted: tired
telegraph: a device for sending messages by radio signals
phonograph: an instrument that used a needle on a record to produce sounds
system: a group of related parts

A Mind for New Ideas

Answer the questions.

1. What is a *patent*? Write your answer in a complete sentence.

   _____

2. Thomas Edison invented all of the following things except

   A. the phonograph.   **B.** the battery.

   C. the automobile.   **D.** the movie camera.

Write **T** for true and **F** for false.

3. _____ Thomas Edison received his first patent for the electric lightbulb.

4. _____ Thomas went to school for 12 years.

5. _____ Thomas Edison wanted to invent things that people could afford to buy.

6. _____ Thomas started his first job when he was 21 years old.

7. _____ Thomas was schooled at home by his mother.

8. Choose the phrase that best completes the sentence.

   Thomas Edison influenced the modern world because he _____.

   A. invented many new things

   B. invented things that we still use today, like the lightbulb and the movie camera

   C. invented so many different things that made use of electricity

   D. B. and C.

9. Thomas's first job was

   A. working in a telegraph office.   **B.** teaching children.

   C. selling things on a train.   **D.** none of the above

10. A phonograph

   A. is like our CD players today.   **B.** played music and voices.

   C. amazed the world when it first came out.   **D.** all of the above

11. Explain what happened next after Thomas Edison invented the lightbulb.

   _____

12. On a separate sheet of paper, write how your day, from getting up to going to bed, would be different if there were no electricity. Use a variety of transitional words, such as *first, then, second,* and *last* to describe your day.

Racing for the Story

Nellie Bly was a **reporter**. This was not a job for a woman in the 1880s. But, Nellie was not afraid to be different. She first went undercover for her stories when she was 18 years old. Once, Nellie got a job in a **factory**. Then, she wrote about how badly the factory workers were treated. She also stayed in a hospital for people with problems. She wanted to see if they were **mistreated**. No job was too hard or too dangerous for Nellie.

In 1873, Jules Verne wrote the book *Around the World in Eighty Days*. People loved the story. In it, a man races around the world to win a bet. In 1888, Nellie's newspaper wanted to send a man on a trip around the world. The man would write about his trip for the paper. Nellie wanted to go. If not, she said, she would write the story for another newspaper.

On the morning of November 14, 1889, Nellie Bly started her trip around the world. She got on a ship that would cross the Atlantic Ocean. She only took one small bag. Women never traveled alone then. But, Nellie was not afraid to make the trip alone.

Nellie's ship stopped in England. It was easy to travel through Europe by train. After that, she traveled by train or boat or carriage. She wrote stories about what she saw. People read and loved her stories.

Nellie's last ship landed in San Francisco, California. There were 12 more days to go. Her train trip across the United States took only four days. Nellie's trip took less than 80 days! It took 72 days, 6 hours, 11 minutes, and 14 seconds. When she got to New York City, there were parades for her. Nellie had raced around the world. And, the whole world knew who she was.

reporter: a person who writes news stories for a newspaper
factory: a building where things are made
mistreated: treated badly

Racing for the Story

Nellie Bly was a **reporter**. This was not a job for a woman in the 1880s. But, Nellie was not afraid to be different. She started going undercover for her stories when she was 18 years old. One time, Nellie got a job in a clothing **factory**. Then, she wrote about how badly the factory workers were treated. She also had herself put into a hospital for people with problems. She wanted to see if they were **mistreated**. No job was too hard or too dangerous for Nellie.

In 1873, Jules Verne wrote the book *Around the World in Eighty Days*. People loved the story about a man who raced around the world to win a bet. In 1888, Nellie's editors wanted to send a man on a trip around the world. The man would write about his trip in the paper. Nellie demanded to go instead. If not, she said, she would write the story for another newspaper.

On the morning of November 14, 1889, Nellie Bly started her trip around the world. She boarded a ship that would cross the Atlantic Ocean. All she took with her was one small purse. Women never traveled alone then. But, Nellie was not afraid to make the trip alone.

Nellie landed in England. It was easy to travel through Europe by train. After that, she made her way by train or boat or carriage. She wrote stories about the sights that she saw. She told about strange clothing and ways. Thousands of people read and loved her stories.

Nellie's ship landed in San Francisco, California, with 12 days to spare. Her train trip across the United States took only four days. Nellie had beaten the 80-day goal! Her trip took 72 days, 6 hours, 11 minutes, and 14 seconds. When she reached New York City, there were parades and fireworks for her. Nellie had raced around the world. And, the whole world knew who she was.

reporter: a person who writes news stories for a newspaper
factory: a building where things are made
mistreated: treated badly

Racing for the Story

Nellie Bly was a reporter. Women **rarely** held newspaper jobs in the 1880s. But, Nellie was not afraid to be different. She started doing undercover work for her stories when she was 18 years old. One time, Nellie got a job in a factory that made clothing. Then, she wrote about the factory's terrible working conditions. She also had herself put into a hospital. She wanted to find out if people with some kinds of health problems were mistreated. No job was too hard or filled with too much danger for Nellie.

In 1873, Jules Verne wrote the book *Around the World in Eighty Days*. People loved the story about a man who raced around the world to win a bet. In 1888, Nellie's editors wanted to send a man on a trip around the world. The man would write about his trip in the paper. Nellie **demanded** to go instead or said she would do it for another newspaper.

On the morning of November 14, 1889, Nellie Bly started her trip around the world. She **boarded** a ship that would cross the Atlantic Ocean. She carried only one small handbag with her. At the time she made her trip, women never traveled alone. But, Nellie was not afraid to make the trip by herself.

Nellie landed in England. It was easy to travel through Europe by train. After that, she had to make her way from train to boat to carriage to finish each part of her trip. She wrote articles about the sights that she saw. She told about strange clothing and **customs**. Thousands of people read and loved her stories.

Nellie's ship landed in San Francisco, California, with 12 days to spare. Her train trip across the United States took only four days. Nellie had beaten the 80-day goal! Her trip took 72 days, 6 hours, 11 minutes, and 14 seconds. When she reached New York City, there were parades and fireworks for her. Nellie had raced around the world. And, the whole world knew who she was.

rarely: not very often
demand: to insist on something
board: get on
customs: ways of behaving that are usual

Racing for the Story

Answer the questions.

1. What is an antonym for *common*?

    A. hilarious   **B.** ordinary   **C.** unusual   **D.** everyday

2. What is *undercover work*?

    A. work done in secret to gather information   **B.** work done in disguise

    C. work done in the open   **D.** A. and B.

3. What inspired the idea of sending someone on an 80-day trip around the world? Write your answer in complete sentences.

    _____

4. Circle three adjectives that describe Nellie Bly.

    timid   serene   stubborn   quaint

    shy   driven   quiet   talented

5. Read the following sentence from the story and answer the question.

    She wrote stories, or articles, about the sights that she saw.

    What is another word or phrase that could replace *articles*?

    A. laws   **B.** research   **C.** novels   **D.** newspaper stories

6. Which of the following best summarizes Nellie's trip?

    A. Nellie Bly traveled around the world.

    B. Nellie Bly beat Jules Verne's fictional record of traveling around the world in 80 days at a time when women did not travel alone.

    C. Nellie Bly was a woman who had done undercover work, so she was not afraid to travel alone.

    D. Nelly Bly traveled around the world, and then people held a parade for her.

7. Which of the following is an opinion?

    A. I think that I would be afraid to travel around the world alone.

    B. Jules Verne wrote the book *Around the World in Eighty Days*.

    C. On the morning of November 14, 1889, Nellie Bly started her trip around the world.

    D. Traveling in Europe in the 1880s was not hard because there were trains.

8. Imagine you are a reporter. Interview a classmate about one or more of the classmate's hobbies. Take notes. Then, write a newspaper story about your classmate on the computer.

Extreme Erosion

The Grand Canyon is one of the natural wonders of the world. It is in the southwestern United States. It was carved out of rock by the Colorado River. It took more than six million years to make this huge canyon. The Grand Canyon is 277 miles (445.79 km) long. It is almost one mile (1.6 km) deep in most places.

Today, the Colorado River runs through the bottom of the Grand Canyon. Visitors can stand on the edge of the canyon. They can see huge striped rocks, hills, valleys, and tall canyon walls. The whole canyon is huge. It is bigger than the state of Rhode Island!

The striped walls of the canyon show layers of rock. The oldest rocks are at the bottom of the canyon. They are almost 2 billion years old. The youngest rocks are at the top of the canyon. They are 270 million years old. **Geologists** have looked at these layers for years. Each layer shows a time in Earth's history. The many different layers cannot be seen so easily anywhere else.

The canyon is also home to more than 2,000 kinds of plants and animals. Many of them are very rare. Some are found only at the Grand Canyon. Many of them are **endangered** or protected.

The Grand Canyon has five different **life zones**. Each life zone is found at a different height. So, each zone has a different kind of weather. And, each zone has a different amount of water. Different plants and animals live in each zone. The Grand Canyon is a rare and extreme place.

geologist: scientist who studies how the earth was formed
endangered: in danger of becoming extinct
life zone: an area made up of specific plant and animal life

Extreme Erosion

The Grand Canyon is one of the natural wonders of the world. It is in the southwestern United States. It was carved out of the rock by the Colorado River. It took more than six million years for the river to make the huge canyon. The Grand Canyon is 277 miles (445.79 km) long. It is almost one mile (1.6 km) deep in most places.

The Colorado River still runs through the bottom of the Grand Canyon. Visitors can stand on one of the rims of the canyon. They can see huge striped rocks, hills, valleys, and **towering** canyon walls. The whole canyon covers more than one million acres (404,685.64 hectares) of land. That is bigger than the state of Rhode Island!

The walls of the canyon are striped. They show layers of rock. The oldest rocks are at the bottom of the canyon. They are almost 2 billion years old. The youngest rocks are at the top of the canyon. They are 270 million years old. **Geologists** have studied these layers for years. Each layer represents a part of time in Earth's history. The Grand Canyon is the only place on the planet where so many different layers can be studied so easily.

The canyon is home to more than 2,000 kinds of plants and animals. Many of them are very rare. Some are found only at the Grand Canyon. Many of them are endangered.

Grand Canyon has five different **life zones**. Each life zone is found at a different **elevation**. So, each zone has a different climate, or type of weather. And, each zone has a different amount of water. All of these things affect the types of plants and animals that can live in each zone of this rare and extreme place.

towering: impressively high or tall
geologist: scientist who studies how the earth was formed
life zone: an area made up of specific plant and animal life
elevation: height above sea level

4.RI.4, 4.RI.10, 4.RF.4, 4.L.4

Extreme Erosion

The Grand Canyon is one of the natural wonders of the world. The gigantic canyon is in the southwestern United States. It was carved out of the rock by the Colorado River. It took more than six million years for the river to make the huge canyon. The Grand Canyon is 277 miles (445.79 km) long, and it is almost one mile (1.6 km) deep in most places.

Today, the Colorado River **snakes** through the bottom of the Grand Canyon. Visitors can stand on one of the rims, or top edges, of the canyon. When they look across, they see huge striped rocks, hills, valleys, and towering canyon walls. The whole canyon covers more than one million acres (404,685.64 hectares) of land. That is bigger than the state of Rhode Island!

The walls of the canyon are striped because they show layers of rock. The oldest rocks are at the bottom of the canyon. They are almost 2 billion years old. The youngest rocks are at the top of the canyon. They are 270 million years old. Geologists, or scientists who study the **formation** of the earth, have studied these layers for years. Each layer represents a part of time in Earth's history. The Grand Canyon is the only place on the planet where so many different layers can be studied so easily.

The canyon is also home to more than 2,000 plant and animal species. Many of them are very rare, and some are found only at the Grand Canyon. Many of the species are endangered or protected.

Because the Grand Canyon is so large and deep, it has five different **life zones**. That means that the canyon has five areas with completely different animals and plants. Each life zone is found at a different **elevation**. So, each zone has a different climate, or type of weather. And, each zone has a different amount of water. All of these things affect the types of plants and animals that can live in each zone of this rare and extreme place.

snake: to follow a twisting path
formation: the act of creating something
life zone: an area made up of specific plant and animal life
elevation: height above sea level

4.RI.1, 4.RI.3, 4.W.3, 4.L.2, 4.L.4

Extreme Erosion

Answer the questions.

1. Which of the following is not a feature of the Grand Canyon?

   A. valleys   **B.** huge striped rocks   **C.** hills   **D.** sand dunes

2. What is a *geologist*?

   A. a scientist who studies dinosaurs

   B. a scientist who studies the formation of stars

   C. a scientist who studies the formation of the earth

   D. a scientist who studies plants and animals

3. Read the following sentence and answer the question.

   Today, the Colorado River snakes through the bottom of the Grand Canyon.

   What is the definition of *snakes* as it is used in this sentence?

   A. winds   **B.** sneaks   **C.** more than one snake   **D.** mean people

4. The Grand Canyon is so huge that it has _____ different life zones.

5. The _____ River carved the Grand Canyon.

6. It took more than _____ years to form the Grand Canyon.

7. The canyon is almost _____ deep in most places.

8. Which of the following is an opinion?

   A. The Grand Canyon is the most beautiful place in the United States.

   B. The Grand Canyon is almost one mile deep.

   C. The Grand Canyon is filled with hills, valleys, and high canyon walls.

   D. Many rare plants and animals live in the Grand Canyon.

9. Why are there so many different life zones in the Grand Canyon? Write your answer in complete sentences.

   _____

   _____

10. On a separate sheet of paper, write about the most beautiful place you have ever visited. Be sure to use correct punctuation, spelling, and capitalization.

Terrific Tides

Can the moon touch Earth? In a way, it does. The moon's gravity pulls on Earth. This is what causes tides. Water moves as the moon travels around Earth. High and low tides are usually a part of everyday life. The water moves only a few feet (a meter), back and forth. But, it's a different story in the Bay of Fundy.

This deep, narrow **bay** is in Nova Scotia, Canada. It is shaped like a **funnel**. The water in the bay moves back and forth all the time. It has the biggest tides in the world. The extreme tides here make the Bay of Fundy known worldwide.

Wolfville is one town on the Bay of Fundy. When the tide is high, fishing boats float on the water. A few hours later, there is no water at all! The **average** difference between high tide and low tide is more than 45 feet (13.72 m) of water. At low tide, boats sit on the mud. People can walk out onto the muddy floor of the bay. Thousands of birds come to eat the small fish left behind by the tide. They also find and eat worms.

When it is time for high tide, look out! More than 100 billion tons (90.72 billion metric tons) of water rush from the ocean. The water pours into the bay in one big wave. The water is so heavy it bends the ground around the bay. In some places, it makes rivers and streams change directions. This is called a tidal bore. A tidal bore is when the incoming tide makes a river or stream go in the opposite direction.

Cape Split is a rocky **cliff** that sticks out into the Bay of Fundy. Here, you can hear a loud roaring sound. It is the sound of the rushing water forcing its way back into the bay. The people who live on the Bay of Fundy say that this noise is "the voice of the moon."

bay: a small body of water set off from the main body
funnel: a device that is shaped like a hollow cone
average: the middle point between two extremes
cliff: a steep overhang, usually of earth or rock

Terrific Tides

Can the moon touch Earth? In a way, it does. The pull of the moon's gravity on the planet is what causes tides. Water moves as the moon travels around Earth. In most places, high and low tides are just a part of everyday life. The water moves only a few feet (a meter), back and forth. But, in the Bay of Fundy, things are different.

This deep, narrow bay is in Nova Scotia, Canada. It is shaped like a **funnel**. The water in the bay moves back and forth constantly with the biggest tides in the world. The extreme tides that are created here make the Bay of Fundy known worldwide.

Wolfville is one town on the Bay of Fundy. When the tide is high, fishing boats float on the water. Just a few hours later, there is no water at all! The **average** difference between high tide and low tide is more than 45 feet (13.72 m) of water. At low tide, boats sit on the mud. People can walk out onto the muddy floor of the bay. Thousands of birds come to eat the small fish and worms left behind by the tide.

When it is time for high tide, look out! More than 100 billion tons (90.72 billion metric tons) of water rush from the ocean into the bay in one big wave. The weight of all of that water actually bends the ground around the bay. In some places, it makes rivers and streams **reverse** directions. This is called a tidal bore. A tidal bore happens when the incoming tide pushes upstream against the usual flow of the water.

Cape Split is a rocky cliff that **juts** into the Bay of Fundy. At this place, you can hear a huge roaring sound. It is the sound of the rushing water forcing its way back into the bay. The people who live on the Bay of Fundy say that this noise is "the voice of the moon."

funnel: a device that is shaped like a hollow cone
average: the middle point between two extremes
reverse: opposite to the usual
jut: to stick out

Terrific Tides

Can the moon touch Earth without a collision? In a way, this actually happens. The tug of the moon's gravity on the planet is what causes tides. Water recedes and advances as the moon travels around Earth. In most places, high and low tides are just an ordinary part of everyday life. The water moves only a few feet (a meter), back and forth, each day. But, in the Bay of Fundy, things are **profoundly** different.

This deep, narrow **inlet** is located in Nova Scotia, Canada. It is shaped like a funnel. The water in the bay fluctuates constantly. The picturesque bay boasts the largest and most varied tides in the world. The extreme tides that are created here bring curious sightseers to the Bay of Fundy from around the globe. Townspeople and international tourists alike gather daily to experience record-setting tides.

Wolfville is one town that is situated along the Bay of Fundy. When the tide is high, fishing boats float on the water. Just a few hours later, there is no water at all! The average difference between high tide and low tide is more than 45 feet (13.72 m) of water. At low tide, boats sit on the mud, grounded. People can wander out onto the muddy floor of the bay. Thousands of birds swoop in to scarf up the small fish and worms left behind by the tide.

Beware of high tide! Then, more than 100 billion tons (90.72 billion metric tons) of water rush from the ocean into the bay in one huge wave. The immense weight of all of that water actually causes the ground around the bay to bend. In some places, it makes adjoining rivers and streams reverse directions. This **phenomena** is called a tidal bore. A tidal bore is the occurrence of an incoming tide that pushes upstream against the usual flow of the water.

Cape Split is a rugged cliff that juts out into the Bay of Fundy. At this place, you can hear a huge roaring sound. It is the **din** of the rushing water forcing its way back into the bay. The inhabitants of the Bay of Fundy say that this noise is "the voice of the moon."

profoundly: in a way that is difficult to understand or explain
inlet: bay, or narrow body of water
phenomena: a rare occurrence
din: sound, noise

Name _____

Terrific Tides

Answer the questions.

1. _____ are made by the pull of the moon's gravity on Earth.

2. One town on the Bay of Fundy is _____.

3. Normal tides change the water level only by _____ .

4. At the Bay of Fundy, the average difference between high and low tide is more than _____ feet (_____ m).

5. Read the sentence from the story and answer the question.

   In most places, high and low tides are just a part of everyday life.

   Which word could replace *everyday* in this sentence?

   A. weekly   **B.** exciting   **C.** engaging   **D.** normal

6. The story mentions all of the following places except

   A. the Bay of Fundy.   **B.** Wolf Cove.   **C.** Cape Split.   **D.** Canada.

7. The title of this story is "Terrific Tides." What is a synonym for *terrific* as it is used in the title?

   A. tremendous   **B.** tiny   **C.** terrible   **D.** trickling

8. The author says that people at the Bay of Fundy call the roaring sound of the tide "the voice of the moon." Why do you think they say this? Write your answer in complete sentences.

   _____

   _____

   _____

9. Look at the drawing. What tide cycle is it on? What else might you see there at this time?

   _____

   _____

   _____

10. Using books, magazines, or the Internet, research the Bay of Fundy. On a separate sheet of paper, write a short essay to tell the new facts you learned about the place. Be sure your essay has an introduction and a conclusion.

Secrets of Giza

Most people know what the Giza Necropolis is. It is where three giant **pyramids** sit on the desert sands of Egypt. Near them is a strange statue. It has the body of a lion and the head of a man. The Giza Necropolis includes the Great Pyramid, two other large pyramids, and several smaller pyramids. The statue near it is the Sphinx. The Great Pyramid is the only ancient wonder still standing today.

Many believe that the pyramids are about 2,000 to 5,000 years old. No one knows for sure. And, no one knows how the pyramids were built. The Great Pyramid alone is made of more than two million stone blocks. Some of the blocks weigh as much as 50 tons (45.36 metric tons)! How did people get them into the desert? The stones may have come up the Nile River on **barges**. **Ramps** could have been used to put each great stone in place. No one knows how long it took to build these huge structures. Some people think that it might have taken 40 years to build one pyramid.

The pyramids are **tombs**. Each pyramid was shaped to look like a stone called a benben. A benben is shaped like a cone. Egyptians thought that the benben stone had special powers because it pointed to the sun and the sky.

The Sphinx is another mystery. Nobody knows who made this strange statue. No one is sure why it is near the tombs. Does it guard the tombs? Some think that the Sphinx's face is really a picture of a great king named Khafre. Khafre was buried in one of the three large pyramids at Giza. Today, scientists are working to find out more. Maybe someday they will know for certain when and how the pyramids and the Sphinx were built.

pyramid: a large structure with a square base and four triangular sides that come to a point at the top

barge: a large boat with a flat bottom

ramp: a sloped floor or walkway

tomb: a place where people are buried

Secrets of Giza

The Giza Necropolis is a familiar sight to many. Three giant **pyramids** sit on the desert sands of Egypt. Near them is an odd statue. It has the body of a lion and the head of a human. The Giza Necropolis includes the Great Pyramid, two other large pyramids, and several smaller pyramids. The statue near it is the Sphinx. The Great Pyramid is one of the Seven Wonders of the Ancient World. It is the only ancient wonder left standing today.

Most scientists believe that the pyramids are about 2,000 to 5,000 years old. How the pyramids were built is a mystery. The Great Pyramid alone is made of more than two million stone blocks. Some of the blocks weigh as much as 50 tons (45.36 metric tons)! How did people get these huge stone blocks into the desert to build the pyramids? The stones may have been brought up the Nile River on barges. **Ramps** were probably used to put each great stone in place. Some scientists think that one pyramid could have taken as long as 40 years to build.

The pyramids are **tombs**. Great kings were buried in them. Each pyramid was shaped like a cone-shaped stone called a benben. The Egyptians thought that the benben stone had special powers because it pointed to the sun and the heavens.

The Sphinx is another mystery. Nobody knows who made this strange statue. No one is sure why it is near the tombs. Does it guard the tombs? Some scientists think that the Sphinx's face is really a **portrait** of a great king named Khafre. Khafre was buried in one of the three large pyramids at Giza. But, other people think that the Sphinx was built first. Today, scientists are working to uncover clues. Maybe someday they will know for certain when and how the pyramids and the Sphinx were built.

pyramid: a large structure with a square base and four triangular sides that come to a point at the top

ramp: a sloped floor or walkway

tomb: a place where people are buried

portrait: a picture or representation of a person

Secrets of Giza

Most people know the Giza Necropolis by sight: three giant pyramids sitting on the desert sands of Egypt. Near them is a strange statue that has the body of a lion and the head of a human. The Giza Necropolis includes the Great Pyramid, two other large pyramids, and several smaller pyramids. The statue near it is the Sphinx. The Great Pyramid is one of the Seven Wonders of the **Ancient** World. It is the only ancient wonder left standing today.

Most scientists believe that the pyramids are about 2,000 to 5,000 years old, but they are not sure. How the pyramids were built is a mystery. The Great Pyramid alone is made of more than two million stone blocks. Some of the blocks weigh as much as 50 tons (45.36 metric tons)! How did people haul these huge stone blocks into the desert to build the pyramids? The stones may have been brought up the Nile River on **barges**. Ramps were probably used to put each great stone in place. Scientists also make guesses about how long it took to build each of these huge **structures**. Some scientists think that each one could have taken as long as 40 years to build.

The pyramids are tombs, or places where great kings were buried. Each pyramid was shaped to look like a **conical** stone called a benben. The Egyptians thought that the benben stone had special powers because it pointed to the sun and the heavens.

The Sphinx is another mystery. Nobody knows who made this strange statue. No one is sure why it is near the tombs. Does it guard the tombs? Some scientists think that the Sphinx's face is really a portrait, or likeness, of a great king named Khafre. Khafre was buried in one of the three large pyramids at Giza. But, other people think that the Sphinx was built first, long before the pyramids and long before Khafre was buried. Today, scientists are working to uncover clues. Maybe someday they will know for certain when and how the pyramids and the Sphinx were built.

ancient: having been around for many years

barge: a large boat with a flat bottom

structure: something that is constructed, often a type of building or shelter

conical: shaped like a cone

Secrets of Giza

Answer the questions.

1. What was the author's purpose in writing this story?

   A. to persuade   **B.** to inform   **C.** to inspire   **D.** none of the above

2. Read the following sentence from the story and answer the question.

   Maybe someday they will know for certain when and how the pyramids and the Sphinx were built.

   Which word could replace *certain*?

   A. forever   **B.** sure   **C.** definitely   **D.** detail

3. List three things that scientists do not know about the structures at Giza.

   _____

   _____

4. Which of the following is the best description of the structures at Giza?

   A. three pyramids and a statue of a lion

   B. four pyramids and a highway

   C. three large pyramids, a statue that has the body of a lion and the head of a human, and several smaller pyramids

   D. one giant pyramid and three small statues

5. What is a *portrait*?

   A. a special building in which a king is buried

   B. a style of building that points to the sun

   C. a likeness of someone's face

   D. a photograph

6. Make a list of at least five two-syllable words and three three-syllable words.

   _____

   _____

7. Read one paragraph of the story aloud to yourself and then to a classmate. Write the name of the classmate here. _____

8. Would you like to visit Giza? Why or why not? Write your answer in complete sentences on another sheet of paper.

Answer Key

Page 7

I. A female clown fish lays 300 to 700 eggs at one time. 2. C; 3. T; 4. F; 5. F; 6. T; 7. F; 8. D; 9. A. tentacles; B. some enemies; C. bait; 10. The clown fish has bright colors and stripes like a clown. II. Answers will vary but should include information to explain the main idea of the story. 12. Answers will vary.

Page 11

I. B; 2. C; 3. C; 4. No one ever saw them perch. 5. Answers will vary but may include: minute, tiny, smallest bird in the world, pea-sized eggs, nest is only about two inches (5.08 cm) wide; 6. D; 7. fast wings, pea-sized eggs, split tongue; 8. Answers will vary but should be in simile or metaphor form. 9. Answers will vary but should include details from the story. 10. Answers will vary but should come from multiple sources.

Page 15

I. B; 2. D; 3. B; 4. B; 5. A; 6. D; 7. C; 8. Answers will vary but should include details from the story. 9. Answers will vary but should include comparisons.

Page 19

I. A yeti is a wild, furry man who lives in the mountains. 2. C; 3. T; 4. F; 5. F; 6. T; 7. F; 8. B; 9. D; 10. B; II. Answers will vary but should include details from the story. 12. Answers will vary. Check for correct spelling, capitalization, and punctuation.

Page 23

I. D; 2. D; 3. Answers will vary but may include: huge, giant, dark, as big as a bus, can swim like a seal, looks like a dinosaur (small head, long neck) 4. model, toy submarine; 5. C; 6. B; 7. Answers will vary. 8. Answers will vary. 9. Answers will vary.

Page 27

I. B; 2. D; 3. Answers will vary but may include: brave, talented, famous, courageous; 4. A; 5. C; 6. B; 7. C; 8. Answers will vary. 9. Answers will vary but should include review and revision.

Page 31

I. B; 2. D; 3. A; 4. A; 5. the *White Knight*; 6. space station; 7. a special type of gas; 8. Answers will vary. 9. Answers will vary but must correlate to answers in question 8. 10. Answers will vary but need to be typed and shared.

Page 35

I. C; 2. D; 3. Answers will vary but may include: Argo is like a big underwater sled. Argo uses sonar to look at the ocean floor and cameras. 4. D; 5. A; 6. C; 7. D; 8. Answers will vary but should incorporate additional research and include an illustration.

Page 39

I. D; 2. Answers will vary but may include: Anne and her family had to hide from the Nazis because they were Jews. 3. A; 4. F; 5. T; 6. F; 7. T; 8. T; 9. Answers will vary but should provide a correct chronology. 10. Answers will vary but should include linking words.

Page 43

I. Gravity; 2. Christmas Day, 1642; 3. learner; 4. kites; 5. grandmother; 6. T; 7. F; 8. F; 9. T; 10. B; II. Answers will vary but must include five or more compound words from the story. 12. Answers will vary but should present an opinion, reasons, and a concluding statement.

Page 47

I. A patent is a notice from the government. It says that someone owns an idea, and it is protected so that others cannot copy it. 2. C; 3. F; 4. F; 5. T; 6. F; 7. T; 8. D; 9. C; 10. D; II. Edison worked to bring lighting to homes, streets, and stores. 12. Answers will vary but must include transitional words.

Page 51

I. C; 2. D; 3. The trip was inspired by Jules Verne's book *Around the World in Eighty Days.* 4. stubborn, driven, talented; 5. D; 6. B; 7. A; 8. Answers will vary.

Page 55

I. D; 2. C; 3. A; 4. five; 5. Colorado; 6. six million; 7. one mile (1.6 km); 8. A; 9. The Grand Canyon has five different life zones because it is so large and deep. The different elevations have different climates, or kinds of weather, and different amounts of water. 10. Answers will vary. Check for correct punctuation, spelling, and capitalization.

Page 59

I. Tides; 2. Wolfville; 3. a few feet (a meter); 4. 45, (13.72); 5. D; 6. B; 7. A; 8. Answers will vary. 9. The tide is out. You might also see people and birds. 10. Answers will vary but must include an introduction and conclusion.

Page 63

I. B; 2. B; 3. Answers will vary but may include: when they were built, how they were built, how long it took to build them; 4. C; 5. C; 6. Answers will vary. 7. Student will read the passage aloud at least twice. 8. Answers will vary but should include the student's opinion and reasons.